Trucks

by Julie Murray

www.abdopublishing.com

Published by Abdo Kids, a division of ABDO, PO Box 398166, Minneapolis, Minnesota 55439.

Copyright © 2015 by Abdo Consulting Group, Inc. International copyrights reserved in all countries. No part of this book may be reproduced in any form without written permission from the publisher.

Printed in the United States of America, North Mankato, Minnesota.

052014

092014

THIS BOOK CONTAINS
RECYCLED MATERIALS

Photo Credits: Getty Images, Shutterstock, Thinkstock,
© bibiphoto p.7, © spirit of america p.15, © Natursports p.21 / Shutterstock.com

Production Contributors: Teddy Borth, Jennie Forsberg, Grace Hansen

Design Contributors: Candice Keimig, Laura Rask, Dorothy Toth

Library of Congress Control Number: 2013953019

Cataloging-in-Publication Data

Murray, Julie.

 Trucks / Julie Murray.

  p. cm. -- (Transportation)

ISBN 978-1-62970-083-0 (lib. bdg.)

Includes bibliographical references and index.

1. Trucks--Juvenile literature.   I. Title.

629.244--dc23

2013953019

Table of Contents

Trucks

Trucks are vehicles

with big engines. They

are very powerful!

4

5

Parts of a Truck

The front of a truck is called the **cab**. The driver sits in the cab.

cab

Different Kinds of Trucks

There are many different kinds of trucks. Tow trucks move cars when they break down.

Fire trucks respond to fires and **emergencies**. They carry ladders and hoses.

Semi-trailer trucks transport **goods**. They carry food, computers, and lots of other things.

Garbage trucks pick up trash.

They crush the garbage and

take it to the dump.

Flatbed trucks have an open, flat **bed**. They carry large items.

Logging trucks are big.

They carry wooden logs.

Monster trucks have big wheels. They can crush cars with their wheels!

21

More Facts

- A semi truck with a full trailer weighs about 80,000 pounds (36,287.4 kg).

- Fire trucks can fit up to 8 fire fighters in full gear inside. A fire fighter's gear weighs about 60 pounds (27.22 kg)!

- Flatbed trucks are one of the most difficult trucks to drive. The trailer does not have any sides. It carries cargo that is too big for regular semi trucks.

Glossary

bed – used to hold large and/or heavy objects and goods.

cab – where the driver sits to control the vehicle.

emergency – a sudden event that requires help or relief.

goods – articles of trade.

vehicle – any means by which to travel. A car is a vehicle. Even a sled is a vehicle.

Index

abdokids.com

Use this code to log on to abdokids.com and access crafts, games, videos and more!

Abdo Kids Code:
TTK0830

24